DECEPTION
on Westminster Bridge, London

That Five Minutes of the Day I Would Want to "Rewind and Erase" from My Memory

Vishnu Mithinti

INDIA • SINGAPORE • MALAYSIA

Notion Press

Old No. 38, New No. 6
McNichols Road, Chetpet
Chennai - 600 031

First Published by Notion Press 2020
Copyright © Vishnu Mithinti 2020
All Rights Reserved.

ISBN 978-1-64828-780-0

I dedicate my first book to my father, the late Prabhakar Ramamurthy, who has never left me in terms of being my inspiration, guide, mentor and philosopher.

This book is especially for the people who want to rewind and erase certain experiences from their life but have not been able to do so.

In that, this book is for all who have experienced or might experience certain events in their lives that they never would want to.

CONTENTS

PART I
THE INCIDENT AND THE IDEA OF
COMING UP WITH A BOOK

PART II
DEALING WITH THE TRAUMA
FROM THE EXPERIENCE

PREFACE

Life has its ways. Events and experiences keep happening throughout our journey from the womb to the tomb. Some, we plan, but most happen without forewarning. Some turn out to be pleasant; their effect remains with us for some time. However, those that are not pleasant stay with us for a long time.

Every one of us has gone through at least one such experience in our life that has troubled our mind for a long time. We do not understand why that experience happened. Or what made us make that decision that caused such a regrettable experience. That which we feel should have never happened in the first place. That which we feel we did not deserve.

The guilt we carry for allowing such an experience to happen in our life is so much that we know it cannot be shared with anyone, nor can we keep it within ourselves. It is both explosive and implosive. It is neither something we can forget nor can we just leave it as some experience in our life.

It is worse when someone else, some stranger, has managed to psyche us to his advantage. When someone has taken control of our mind, our ego, our actions, our reactions and everything that we thought no one else in this world can take control of. Even if it was for just a few minutes, it was enough to shatter our ego and our confidence in our self-control.

It is even worse when it happens in front of one of our dear ones. Someone who looks up to us as an idol, as a mentor, as someone who could never be a victim to such a blunder. They watch, they are also drawn into it, they also participate. And then they are also in the same boat as you are in, experiencing the incident the same way that you are—shocked, regretful, guilty, with a shattered ego and plummeting self-confidence.

I am writing this book to narrate this un-shareable, unforgettable, unforgivable, unimaginable experience of my life, or shall I say, our life (my daughter's, her friend's and mine).

I am a middle-aged man now, having served in one of the elite arms of the Indian Defence Forces for twenty-four years. I have travelled all around the country in my years of service. For the last seven years, I have served as a trainer on life skills at various institutes. Given these credentials, I find it difficult to digest what happened that day on Westminster's Bridge.

WHY SHOULD I BE WRITING A BOOK?

Well, to share it, to forgive and to accept it just as it happened, without any strings, like regret, guilt, remorse and the likes, attached to it.

Another reason is to help others who have had a similar experience in their life and would want to ***"rewind and erase"*** from their memories and from their lives. Also, to relate with those who had a certain experience they wished should never happen to them.

And lastly, to find a way out from the relentless bombardment of thoughts that do not allow us to do anything else effectively and efficiently. That is, to find a solution on how to manage such an unwelcome experience so that life is taken as it comes and deal with such incidents more powerfully.

In helping to get this book out, my daughter, Shraddha, has been a great source of encouragement. Not only did she experience this event along with me, but she was also the first proofreader and editor of this book. The second person to have read the manuscript was my son, Pradyumna, who came laughing to me and said teasingly, "Dad, seriously? How could you get duped like that?" And then it became clear to me that the most important person in my life, my wife, Krishnaveni, would be the third person to know about this experience but only when I get it printed and gift her the first copy.

INTRODUCTION

When I pushed myself into experiencing an event, which turned into an embarrassing, traumatising experience, I just did not know how to deal with it. I couldn't tell anyone. Except for the two who went through the experience with me, I could not share it with anyone else, let alone write a book about it. I did not share it with my wife or even with my close friends. It would have been like telling them, "Look, what a big idiot I am!"

But then here I am writing a book on it. Narrating it. Reliving it. Not wanting to forget it, but wanting to accept it. As soon as I sobered down from the initial shock, all that occurred to me was to do something about it. I did not know what but something that would not make me sulk about it. That would, instead, transform me into a stronger individual than someone who felt victimised.

The first thing I wanted to do was to stand on top of the world and shout, "Look, I know I have blundered. So what? I am human."

That's it. No more. No less. I am human. Is that, that difficult to accept? I don't think so.

The second thing that occurred to me was how I should deal with it.

Lastly, it was about telling people how to deal with it.

That's it. That's why this book.

Now, one might ask, after this effort, has it transformed me?

Well, if, from feeling "Why has this happened to me?" or "How did I allow this to happen to me?" to "This is an opportunity for me to introspect and tell people how to deal with such experiences" can be termed as transformation, then YES, it has transformed me.

The trauma from the experience has now changed to excitement in writing this book. Well, this also is transformation, isn't it?

The negative bombardments in the mind are replaced by positive ideas about how to write about dealing with such incidents. Isn't that too a transformation?

Narrating the incident straightaway would not make much sense if I don't give a brief introduction about myself and others who were, shall I say, victims of the incident?

Well, I am a middle-aged (fifty-four years to be precise) man from Hyderabad, India, whose daughter was pursuing her master's in London. She had left three months before I visited her. She began her master's degree in the first week of September 2018, and I went to visit her in November of the same year. In fact, I had booked my tickets to visit her between the 15th and 21st of November. But due to certain reasons, which I shall go through later, I had to cancel my visit. I was unsure if I should rebook my tickets.

But then, not willing to give up and to keep my daughter's spirits high, after consulting my doctor,

I decided to make the trip from 29 November 2018, a little later than intended originally. I bought the tickets only for the onward journey, hoping that I could purchase return journey tickets from there at a low price. It did not happen that way, though.

It is time I gave myself a name. My name is Vishnu, and I am from a place called Hyderabad in India. My daughter's name is Shraddha.

I reached London on the evening of 29th November. My daughter came to pick me up from the airport. It was a great reunion, albeit in just three months. She welcomed me with a big affectionate hug. We moved towards the underground tube station as she felt that was the best way to go during that hour of the day when office-goers would choke the roads.

The moment we stepped out of the airport into the tube station, I got the first bite of London's weather. A chill breeze hitting my face. I immediately put on the cap she gave me and covered my ears. I also adorned myself with a neck collar that my doctor asked me to put on at all times.

We reached her room at North Acton in London. She told me I could stay with her in her room for not more than three days. It was fine, as we had planned to go to my wife's cousin's place a day later.

Well, three days went by happily meeting people and going around her college and London. When we shifted to my wife's cousin's place, my daughter's friend from Middleborough decided to come and meet us. Her name is Diya. She was also from our place and had completed her under graduation at Hyderabad, along with my daughter. And she too had decided to do her master's in the UK. Her college was in Middleborough. After coming to the UK, these two girls had not met each other. Since I had also come to London, she decided to come and stay with us for two days.

As we couldn't stay at my daughter's hostel, we decided to hire accommodation through an Airbnb website. We selected a place somewhere near Central London.

Her friend reached London at about nine in the morning on Monday, 3rd December 2018, from Middleborough. We met her at the tube station and had a quick bite at McD. The check-in time at the accommodation was after 4 p.m. We had a lot of time to go around London. We collected an Oyster card for Diya and decided to go around London until at least 3:30 p.m. We set course towards the London museum and went around the place. We took some snaps there. Then my daughter asked if we could go to Westminster Bridge.

Not knowing what lay in store for us, we said, "Let's go."

We reached the Westminster Bridge, and the girls were taking a few snaps here and there. I went over to the Westminster Bridge and stood waiting for them. They joined me but were still in their world of taking snaps and selfies.

That's when I saw 'them.' That is when the "DECEPTION" took place. That is where I was tricked like never before. That is where I, we, had the worst experience of our lives. As I write this, my hands are still shaking with the thought of the incident. However, I am determined to write about this and want to deal with it head-on.

I have this book written in two parts.

Part I deals with the incident, the immediate aftermath and the idea of coming out with a book.

Part II deals with how to deal with such experiences and how I dealt with it.

THE INCIDENT AND THE IDEA OF COMING UP WITH A BOOK

DECEPTION: THE INCIDENT

On the 3rd of December 2018, my daughter, her friend and I were exploring the area in London near Westminster Bridge. It was about 3 p.m. when I was casually walking over the beginning of the Westminster Bridge from the clock tower side, and something caught my attention. Ignoring it, I looked around for the two girls. I saw them, my daughter and her friend, taking selfies and snaps on the other side of the road.

I paused on the middle of the road at the beginning of the bridge and looked all around again. Something unusual caught my attention again. I noticed two men walking towards me from the side of the bridge. One was wearing a grey-coloured coat with a cap, and the one behind him was a short, stout, fair man with short, curly brown hair. He was wearing blue-coloured jeans and a T-shirt. The other man had a cigarette in his hand.

The fair stout man with curly hair stopped at a place indicated by the other man and looked around. I was wondering what they were up to. Just then, the man with the brown curly hair took out a small piece of yellow cloth of about one foot by one and a half feet and spread it on the floor near the side of the bridge. The man with the cigarette appeared to be saying, "Yes, this is an ok place."

The man who spread the cloth then took out three small metallic conical cups. They looked like small cups to hold as a toast with wine in it. Only these were aluminium-coloured metallic ones. He placed the three cups upside down over the cloth in a horizontal line.

He then took out what looked like a small lime. No, it was lime. He placed the lime inside the first cup and, again, placed it upside down such the lime was trapped inside the cup.

I found it very amusing and thought, *Ok, this guy is up to some trick.* I started watching him keenly.

He bent down, showed the cup with the lime, and moved it around the other cups as if he were juggling. While moving the cups with both hands, he lifted the cup with the lime and shifted it into another cup. He did like this a few times and then started asking a small group surrounding him which cup the lime was in.

The man with the cigarette who was standing near me stepped forward and pushed open the middle one. Even I knew it wasn't in that. The man who was juggling asked him to give money. Then the man beside me gave him maybe ten pounds and opened the middle one. I was about to tell him it wasn't in that, but it was too late. He opened it, and it was not in that. He was disappointed, obviously, and I thought he was not attentive enough.

I knew where the lime was and smiled to myself, looking at the cup under which I was sure it was. The man on the floor was still asking people to guess which of the remaining two it was in. A man opposite me, who was wearing a cap, came forward and opened the cup that was facing me. And I knew it was not in that too. He opened it, and he was disappointed that it wasn't in that too.

So, my guess was right. It was in the third one.

The juggler started the game again. I was very keenly watching him, and when he stopped, I knew exactly where the lime was.

A man in front of the juggler, who was to my right, came forward, gave him some money and kicked the cup in the centre of the lineup. Oops! He was hugely disappointed.

I knew exactly where it was. I just looked around for my daughter to show her how smart I was. She was standing near me. I called and told her, "Just see how he is fooling people. He is juggling the lime inside the cups and asking people to guess where, in which cup it is." And then I told her that out of the remaining two, it was inside the third one opposite where we were standing. I told her, "Just keep watching what happens."

Just then, the man beside me with the cigarette came forward, gave him some money, went to open the third one, and opened it. And lo! It was there.

I said to my daughter, "See, I knew it was there. Actually, if we watch keenly, we can easily make out where it is." She agreed and smiled.

Just then, her friend Diya joined us. We told her what happened. And now the three of us were watching the juggling intently.

Again, he juggled the three cups with the lime in one of them, changing it from one into another. But it was very easy to watch where it was moving from where we were standing. I had chosen a very strategic position, I thought proudly. He stopped and asked people where it was. The man opposite to us came again and kicked one of the cups that I was sure it was not in. There were two more cups left, and I knew for sure that it was in the cup closer to me.

I looked at my daughter and told her, "I am sure it is here in this cup," pointing to the cup near us.

She agreed and said, "Yes, it is there."

I then took out my purse, pulled out a twenty-pound note and stepped forward reluctantly. The juggler looked at me and stepped forwarded and shouted, "COME ON, COME ON, WHERE IS IT? WHERE IS IT?" I noticed now that he was not English.

I showed him the first cup near me and said, "This" and gave him the twenty-pound note.

And then, this is what happened.

The man standing beside me towards my right came very near me, peeped into my purse, and shouted, "NO, GIVE FIFTY. GIVE FIFTY. IT IS THERE. I KNOW. I KNOW. YOU ARE RIGHT. GIVE FIFTY, FIFTY."

I did not even look at him properly. I was smiling at my confidence and glad that someone else also felt it was in the same cup.

And then I gave fifty pounds. I vaguely remember taking back the twenty I gave.

The man came close again and started shouting in my ear, "NO. GIVE HUNDRED. IT IS THERE ONLY. I KNOW. I KNOW. YOU ARE RIGHT. GIVE HUNDRED. GIVE, GIVE, GIVE." He kept gesturing as though he was giving it away. He kept shouting the same thing repeatedly.

I did not even get time to think. And then I gave another fifty.

He came close again and started shouting even more loudly, almost hysterically, "NO, NO. GIVE MORE. GIVE TWO HUNDRED. GIVE ANOTHER HUNDRED. GIVE, GIVE, GIVE. GIVE THAT FIFTY, GIVE THAT FIFTY." His hands were moving hysterically from my purse to the juggler, gesturing to me to give.

There was no time to think. But Shraddha, my daughter, for a brief moment, could think. She asked that man, "Why don't you give? You put."

He looked at her and said, "No money, no money. Your daddy has. Give, give, give." He came near me and told in my ear, "*Keep your leg on the cup. Keep, keep your leg; otherwise, he will change. Come on, come on, keep, keep, keep your leg.*"

I kept my leg over the inverted cup.

He kept encouraging non-stop, I think instigating is a better word, so much that I could not even think straight.

And then I gave another fifty.

He was still close to me and said, "NO, NO. GIVE FIFTY. GIVE THAT FIFTY ALSO. GIVE TWO HUNDRED. GIVE, GIVE, GIVE."

I could see my daughter's reluctant hand over my purse, murmuring, "Daddy, Daddy, shshshshs…wait."

Suddenly, I halted. I stopped this fellow and told the juggler, "Give me those 150 pounds. Give it back."

The man beside me who was instigating me said, "Ok, ok. Enough," and signalled for the juggler to go. He then asked me to remove the cup. "Open, open. See, see. Open it."

I bent forward and opened it confidently without any hesitation.

And… "OH MY!" was all I could utter.

My daughter held her hand to her chest and with big, surprised wide eyes said, "Oh! Dad!"

My heart sank. And I got up not knowing what hit me. **The lime wasn't inside the cup.** That meant I had lost about 150 pounds in just a few minutes.

Shocking! Shocking! Unbelievable.

I did not know what to do and how to react. I just took two steps behind. My daughter was to my left, holding my arm tightly. Her friend was to my right. I did not even dare to look at them.

The juggler continued with his juggling as though nothing had happened. Not knowing where to look, we were looking at his juggling actions. So clever. So adept. All the three of us were keenly observing the movement of his hand, as though trying to find out where we went wrong. He stopped the juggling and kept his palm over two of the three turned-down cups. He was asking people which cup the lime was lying in. We three could very clearly make out into which cup the lime went.

I told my daughter, "Look. It is clearly in the third one. The one opposite to us."

To this, both she and her friend replied, "Yes, it is in there in the third cup for sure."

The man standing opposite us kicked the centre cup as though telling us, "Look, you are right. It is not in the middle one."

Now, only two cups were remaining, and we knew where it was.

This time, my daughter's friend said, "Uncle, I am sure it is in the third one."

"Are you sure?" I asked her to confirm again if she also thought the same.

She said, "Yes, uncle."

I reiterated, "Yes, it is there."

My daughter also confirmed, "I am sure it is there."

The two girls stepped forward.

The man beside me to my right looked at them and said, "Yes, yes. Go there. Go there. Stand there."

They went obediently and stood near the third cup opposite me. I took out my purse, which I had put in my pocket, promising not to take it out, at least until we left this place. I took out a twenty-pound note but was searching for a ten-pound note. The man to my right came near me and was at his best again, shouting, instigating.

"GIVE, GIVE, GIVE. GIVE HUNDRED. GIVE TWO HUNDRED." This time, he added, "TAKE BACK YOUR MONEY. YOU ARE RIGHT. YOU ARE RIGHT. IT IS THERE IN THE THIRD CUP. GIVE, GIVE."

Now, he did something more.

While the juggler was to my left asking the man beside me where the lime was, the man to my right bent forward towards the cups. As though doing it clandestinely, out of the two cups left out to be checked, he tilted the first cup that was towards me, looked at me, and said, "Look, it is not there. That is the one." He gestured towards my daughter and her friend and said, "Keep your leg over it, keep your leg on it."

Both of them kept their legs on the tiny cup as though telling the juggler, "This time, we won't let it go. We will get back our money."

I was still holding on to the twenty-pound note. I was looking at the girls.

The man to my right came to me and was at it again. "GIVE, GIVE, GIVE. GIVE FIFTY. GIVE HUNDRED."

I took out another twenty. The juggler was in front of me to collect the money.

"GIVE, GIVE. TAKE OUT MORE. TAKE YOUR MONEY BACK. GIVE HUNDRED," the man to my right was almost yelling.

I took out more money and gave the girls one last look.

My daughter showed confidence but was scared too. Her friend gestured with her hand and assured by closing her eyes and whispering, "Don't worry, Uncle. I am more than confident. It is here only."

I shelled out another hundred pounds.

The man was still shouting. "MORE, MORE, MORE."

I almost shouted, "I DON'T HAVE ANYMORE."

He took pity and moved away.

My daughter and her friend together confidently overturned the cup.

And…and…

There was nothing there…

We were shell-shocked. Totally stunned. Bewildered. Mystified. I can add many more such synonyms from the thesaurus, but none would match the actual feelings we felt there.

The two girls came hurriedly towards me, almost shouting, "How is that possible? I saw it in that. That's impossible."

They were beside me. Both. One at each side. My daughter was holding my hand, almost shivering.

All three of us were silent. What could we say, though?

We were looking right through them, dazed and in shock.

Suddenly, we noticed that the juggler put the cups in his coat. He took the cloth from the floor and put it in his pocket. And all of them walked out together in the direction opposite to where we were standing. We did not know what was happening. They were gone in a jiffy.

Diya said, "Uncle, they just went away."

I looked in that direction and saw that they had vanished.

We were standing there like fools. Shell-shocked. Not knowing what just hit us. Totally baffled. Paralysed.

Life was going on as usual in that path of the Westminster Bridge. People walking to and fro. Everything appeared normal. The place where the juggling was done also was filled with people walking on the bridge. We were the only ones standing, somewhat in the centre, as though not knowing what to do. Which side to walk. Unable to come to terms with what just happened. But what happened? Where did it happen? Everything around us looked so normal, but our minds were exploding with thoughts, with regret, with guilt, with shame, with shock, with sadness.

More than 200 pounds in just five minutes. Puffff… into thin air. I am unable even to dare to confess that if one does the maths, it is much more than that, that I blew in just a few minutes.

So much turmoil within, yet so much normalcy outside. Was this a dream? A nightmare?

Suddenly, I heard my daughter's voice, which had the tone of shock, sadness and curiosity, "Dad, how much did you give?"

I came to my senses, turned around with the two girls close on my heels and said, "Don't even ask. Forget about it. Let us forget what has just happened. I don't want us to bother about it. Let's just go from here."

I looked around. No one was looking at us or sympathising with us. Because none of those people were there. The man encouraging me had also vanished.

Then it struck me and struck me hard.

All these guys were together. The juggler, the man who was to my left. The man who was to my right instigating me. And also the man opposite me to the other end. And maybe there were more. All were together. A team. A gang, of sorts.

All played together. One was juggling, and others were giving money and acting as though they were also playing. Sometimes winning, sometimes losing, but getting their money back for sure. One was instigating, no, psyching. Yes, *psyching* is the right word.

He just did not allow me to think, to look around. Just kept shouting, shouting and shouting over my ears. And I fell for it. Like I was under his spell. And kept doing what he asked me to do.

Something else struck me at that time. In the last game, all three were empty. One was kicked by the man standing opposite. The man to my right opened and showed the first one. And the girls lifted the last one. Where was the lime then?

Oh, God! We had been tricked! Tricked! Absolute cheating!

PERFECT DECEPTION.

I could not imagine that what started as a ridiculous amusement ended up so disastrously for me. For us, rather. And all within a few minutes. Everything appeared so conscious yet so unconscious.

Conscious actions with an unconscious mind. Or is it the other way round? Unconscious actions with (their) conscious mind. Because it appeared as though

my mind had gone into hibernation or, more aptly, under subjugation.

I had never gambled like this in my life. But was this gambling? It was not supposed to be. It was supposed to be some small trick by some foreigners showing off their skills in a tourist city while some innocent, unsuspecting tourists got involved for some fun. That was it. But what has this resulted in? A nightmare for some and grand fun for some others? All this was running in my mind while we were just walking silently towards the first bus stop we could find. We reached there and silently waited for the bus.

My daughter's friend looked behind and found some shop there. She said, "I will just go and buy something to eat."

She was back in a few minutes. She called me and was trying to give me something saying, "Uncle, please take this."

I looked at her palm. There were some pound notes.

I said, "What is this? Don't be silly."

She said, "It is 100 pounds. Please don't say no. Please take it, Uncle. Else, I will feel very guilty. After all, we played the last one because of me. I was very confident that it was there."

I looked at her. I wanted to laugh. I wanted to shout, "Our fault?"

Instead, I just said, "Don't worry about that. And I cannot take this. Not from you. And don't worry about the last game. It was, in fact, I who dragged you girls into it in the first place. Just keep the money inside. And let us discuss it later in the room. Keep it inside."

She kept the money inside, and we waited for the bus in silence. It looked like an eternity before the bus arrived. We changed two buses to reach our destination, the flat booked through Airbnb. En route, I kept telling them that this was something we needed to forget.

"We won't be able to, but just accept it as some nightmare and leave it where it happened, on the Westminster Bridge. Let's not carry it with us," I repeated to them as though telling myself loudly.

Easy to say but very difficult to follow. I could easily make out that the incident was playing havoc in the three of our minds. But there was nothing we could do. Nothing much I could do.

After we checked into the room, we heated the snacks we got for dinner and had them.

When my daughter went to the washroom, I told Diya, "Just try and get it out of your mind and relax. Try not to keep recollecting it."

She said, "Uncle, I just cannot understand how he did it. How could we get cheated so badly?" All I could do was tell her not to think about it much.

After my daughter came in, I suddenly, for some reason, told her that I would be leaving on 6th December, instead of the 8th, as I had planned earlier. She, for some reason, did not disapprove and said, "Let's check the rates." Until then, she wanted me to stay at least until the 8th of December. We started checking for rates on various websites.

Meanwhile, we called up our relative who had kept my suitcase in his office. Since his office was nearby, he was to bring the suitcase to the room after we reached there in the evening. After he came with the suitcase, we chatted a bit. We told him nothing about the incident. How could we? He left after a while.

I telephonically booked my ticket for the 6th evening by Jet Airways. I tried my best not to allow the thought, *Was I running away…from something?*

We relaxed a bit and then decided to sleep. Our minds were in turmoil. We experienced what we had never experienced before—cheating, submission, shock, cunningness, losing control of self to a stranger, anger, shame, guilt, helplessness over deception.

When I got up in the morning, the first thing that came into the mind was the small three cups, the lime and his cunning juggling and that fellow shouting in my ears.

Oh! How I hated this first thought of the morning.

The next day, we went around London and 'enjoyed' ourselves. At night, Diya left for Middleborough. My daughter and I came back to the room and slept.

Before sleeping, my daughter said, "Dad, it does not go from the head. I just do not like the thought that he cheated us."

I hugged her and forced a smile. Like every loveable daughter, she also thought that her dad was immune to anything bad. This was probably the first shock in her life that 'her dad, after all, is no hero.'

Well, I thought, *Yes, darling, your dad is a mere mortal with the same weakness and vulnerabilities as anyone else.* I hated this thought.

Surprisingly, I slept well. But I got up the next day with the same thought of what happened that day, a bit less vividly though.

Time has started to play its role, I thought and smiled. The next two days went off well. We went around seeing more of London. We went to her bank and deposited some money into her account. We did some shopping, cautiously, though.

We probably talked about it one more time when my daughter again expressed her agony of not liking someone duping her father. I told her to stop thinking that way and just imagine "how we would treat this event six months from now." She later told me that this did give her some comfort.

Finally, the day to leave London had arrived. My daughter came to the airport to see me off. She put up a brave front, not showing her sadness that I was leaving. As soon as I collected my boarding pass, I had coffee with her. Then I bid her bye and went inside.

I spoke to her once I got into the flight and then put my phone on in-flight mode.

As soon as the flight took off, my neighbour got into a conversation with me. Apparently, he was also a trainer. So, I felt comfortable chatting with him.

I felt like sharing my experience with him. After some time, on some pretext, I shared it. But I could only share that some terrible experience happened to me on the Westminster Bridge and how I took it in stride. I told him about how I told my daughter and her friend on how to deal with it. How it should be accepted as some event that has happened and not reason with it. And how it is to be left where it is and not carried with us to the future in our minds. I told him how I dealt with it courageously and was moving on with life.

He seemed to have believed what I said, but somehow, I did not believe it myself. It gave me some relief, but that was not enough. Something was missing there. Was I scared to share it completely? Was I running away from it? Why was feeling uncomfortable within? Did I really accept what happened as something that happened and that's all? Nothing to worry about, nothing to brood over, nothing to feel ashamed of, nothing to feel guilty about? I don't think so.

Suddenly, I got bored with the gentleman sitting beside me and yapping away. I took a break and told him, "I am feeling sleepy and want to sleep for half an hour." After that, I did not speak to him until we landed in Mumbai.

In Mumbai, I went through the immigration, took my boarding pass to board the flight to Hyderabad and boarded my flight at 0410 hrs.

I slept in the flight for about half an hour and woke up with the event playing in my mind. I had the snacks they served and waited for the aeroplane to land at Hyderabad. After it landed at about 0600 hrs, I took my luggage and came out.

I had some coffee outside and decided to take the Pushpak, the airport bus from the airport to a stop near my house. The bus started fifteen minutes after I boarded it. The incident popped up in my mind again. I was wondering, *Now that I am home, how should I go about it?*

But before that, let me take you through the tsunami of thoughts that I was being pounded with.

THE THOUGHTS AFTER THE INCIDENT

How has this incident affected me, or how will it affect me in the future? What were the thoughts that were bombarding me, non-stop?

It would rather be unfair to the girls to say that this incident affected only me. They were equally affected. Maybe more. That's because they had hardly yet seen the outside world and this must have come as a rude shock at a pretty early age of 23. I have lived for about 54 years and have travelled extensively. I have seen the world, have been cautious about life and its ways. Still, this particular event shook me in a way I haven't experienced till date.

Why is this incident disturbing me so much? What impacted me the most? Let me check.

Is it shock?

Is it disbelief?

Is it that my ego got battered?

Is it my impulsive decision?

Is it my inability to foresee the deceit?

Is it that it happened in front of my daughter and her friend?

Is it surrender to my temptation or greed?

Is it that I fell to gambling so easily?

Is it the loss of money in just a few minutes?

Is it that someone else, particularly a stranger, took control of my mind and actions? Is it that I am so vulnerable?

Is it that I did not know how to handle it?

Is it that I cannot share it with anyone for the rest of my life?

The powerful mind is capable of brewing innumerable such thoughts, mostly negative, in a very short period. But putting them down is meaningless and doesn't serve much purpose.

All of the above and more similar thoughts impacted my mind immediately and for some time after the incident occurred. And I knew I had to do something about it—something that would free my mind from the huge burden of such thoughts and their impact on me. Something that would break the silence, which was stirring a storm of thoughts and silent dialogues between my daughter and me, and her friend too. This noisy silence in us had to be broken.

And I felt the only way to do it is to transform it into something—I didn't know into what. But into something that leaves a positive impact rather than a negative one.

Initially, as soon as we started moving from there, I tried my best to make them feel comfortable and not to overthink.

I even stopped discussing it later with my daughter. But sure enough, every time I spoke to her over video chat, which happened almost daily, I saw that look on her face that, I felt, read as, "Oh, Pops! Why did this happen to us? I feel so bad for us. Why the hell did I insist on you coming here to London and spending time with me? I am so sorry about what happened!"

And when I was speaking with her, during the same video chat, I was saying something else, while I actually wanted to say, "That's ok, dotty darling. Take it easy. It happens. Don't worry about the money. By God's grace, I have the ability to take that much of monetary shock, at least. So far as other things are concerned, just forget about it. Don't let it bother you too much. Just focus on what you are there for and enjoy life."

Such experiences cannot be erased from our mind, and one should never even try to do so. Because the more we try to erase or forget, the more intensely they come back to our mind. And we would feel more traumatised every time. As a result, it slowly gets firmly established in our mind and pops up at every opportunity.

It is not that only negative, self-pitying or confusing thoughts occurred. There were flashes of positive thoughts, as well. Like…

Has this occurred to teach me something about me, about life and its ups and downs? And is it giving me an opportunity to learn how to handle it?

Had this not occurred, maybe something more disastrous would have happened.

Such an event would caution the young girls of life's unpredictability in an otherwise happy-go-lucky, easy-going life of theirs.

Maybe this has happened so that I can caution people about such fortuitous incidents in our lives, which 'we want to reverse or erase,' and how to tackle them.

THE IDEA OF WRITING A BOOK

After reaching Hyderabad, I took the airport bus home. The bus had run for about fifteen minutes when I got this **idea, a brilliant one**—to do what I was afraid to do. To tell people what happened. And the only one way I could do that is by writing about it. To write about my experience. **To write a book**, maybe. To write vividly how it happened. To write if we can prevent such things happening to us.

I was very excited about the idea. I felt really good as if I knew exactly what to do about this.

Suddenly, the two girls came into my mind. *What about them?* I thought.

And immediately, from my side, I had an answer to that too. My daughter was doing her masters in animation. So she could make an animation clip or a short movie on the whole incident. Her friend was an excellent artist and could sketch very well. So she could draw sketches or illustrations on the entire incident. When or whether they did, it was up to them. But I was sure that this was the only way they also could 'accept' things as they were and move forward in life more powerfully. However, I had to leave it to them to decide how they wanted to handle it.

I was very excited about what I wanted to do. And every time I thought about this, the excitement grew. I realised that the incident and its effect took a back seat and writing about it and sharing how to tackle such events in our life, which we sometimes want to "**rewind and erase,**" was in the forefront of my mind.

Of all the positive thoughts, what stuck with me most is this.

This happened so that I bring it out and caution people of life's cruel jokes at times and share with them how I felt it should be handled. This will also transform the guilt, the shame, the loss and the bashed-up ego into something positive.

Wow! I found a way to transform this event from trauma to excitement. From shock to expressions. From guilt to acceptance. That's how this event took the form of a book. I was wondering what to write in the book, apart from the incident itself. Ever since I got this idea of writing about the incident, I started working out what should be written.

First, obviously, it had to be the incident itself. Secondly, it would be the tsunami of thoughts that kept bombarding from within. But that would only be something like sharing an experience and the turmoil from within with everyone. But of what use would it be to anyone? Maybe a few would draw some lessons from it. But for most, it would just be somebody else's experience. Some might even wonder how anyone can get into such a silly trap.

I wasn't sure what to write until I actually starting writing. And when I started writing, slowly, it started becoming clear what all should be written. That excited me even more.

And that is how Part II, the important part of the book, emerged.

PART II

DEALING WITH THE TRAUMA FROM THE EXPERIENCE

THE THREE STAGES IN OUR LIFE'S EXPERIENCES

Our entire journey from the time we land in the crib to the time we lie down on the pyre is full of experiences. We plan and enjoy some of these experiences. Some happen without any planning. Yet others just happen; we don't know why. Some give us happiness while some inflict pain. From some, we learn, while a few, we regret.

All these experiences have an effect on us. The intensity of the effect on us depends on the impact of the experience on our body and mind. Very often, regrettable experiences have a stronger impact than joyful ones. And these are the ones that we get stuck with for a long time. Hence, it is important to deal with these regrettable experiences since they generally have a negative effect on us.

All such experiences that we face have three phases or stages.

The **first stage** is before they occur or are likely to occur.

The **second stage** is when we are experiencing them.

And the **third stage,** after it has occurred and impacted our life severely. Physically and/or mentally and/or emotionally. This is when we desperately hope that these experiences which, given a chance, we would want to *"REWIND AND ERASE"* from our life, from our memories.

So that's what needs to be addressed. How do we deal with such incidents—before, during and after? That is, recognising them before they occur, pulling out while they are occurring and after they have occurred and impacted our lives, dealing with the aftermath. And what do we need to know about these stages?

FIRST STAGE

Recognising the warnings before they occur. Before such incidents cause a shocking, everlasting impression in our lives, can we avoid them? Can something warn us when such experiences are likely to happen?

Yes. One does get warnings, it is said. But we have to train ourselves to be extraordinary and supernatural human beings who understand certain warnings from the "elements" in the universe, which would make us feel conscious of some uncomfortable feeling (gut feeling) that something terrible is likely to happen. Well, the fact is, it is not possible for all.

Most of us are normal, simple humans who cannot develop such powers. But then, once we have decided to get ourselves into certain situations, knowingly or deliberately, we can make a conscious decision to avoid turning such incidents into traumatic experiences.

How? That should be explored, and I intend to dwell on that.

SECOND STAGE

Can we alert ourselves and withdraw in time while we are in the middle of some traumatic experience? Let us say we have dived into such situations. How can we try to get out in the middle of it? That is, halfway through experiencing it. That would be my next area to ponder on.

THIRD STAGE

How to deal with such experiences that have already impacted us? Now, we have dived into it, got drowned, choked ourselves but surfaced somehow. What to do with such traumatising, suffocating experiences in life? It will not allow us to breathe properly for the rest of our lives. So, I would explore ways to emerge out of such experiences more powerfully, more positively. See how to deal with it in a manner that it is transformed into something more positive or at least into an experience of learning, if nothing else.

FIRST STAGE

RECOGNISING THE WARNINGS BEFORE A TRAUMATIC EXPERIENCE OCCURS

Can one really get a warning before any such experiences are likely to happen, particularly, the traumatising ones? Is it possible?

We have read about telepathy, clairvoyance, sixth sense, ESP (Extra-Sensory Power), etc., which some people have mastered and enable them to foresee certain happenings in their life. There are some occult sciences like palmistry, astrology and numerology, which predict both good and bad in our lives. But how accurate they are, it is not for me to say. These require training for many years before anyone can claim to possess such powers. It is beyond the scope of us ordinary human mortals who live simple lives of experiencing things as they happen.

Talking about getting a forewarning about such experiences, there is one thing worth sharing here about this London trip of mine in November 2018.

I still am wondering, was it a pre-warning for something big to happen? I do not know, and I realise that there is no way to know either. But read on. It is interesting, though.

My initial plan was to go to London on 15th November and return on 21st November 2018. But something happened on the 11th of November due to which I had to cancel my tickets, which I had booked almost three months in advance.

Another traumatic experience might be a laughable one but is worth sharing nevertheless.

On the 11th of November at about 6 a.m, I had gone to my barber for a haircut. After the haircut, I asked him for a hair oil massage. He massaged my hair and then asked if he should twist my head. They do this by standing behind the client and putting one hand over the head and the other under the chin. They then check if the client's neck has loosened and then give a sudden twist to the left and then to the right. It gives a 'crrrick' kind of sound at the neck.

Initially, I refused and was getting off the chair. Something came over me, and I sat back, asking him to do it, anyway. He checked for the looseness of my neck and gave the jerky twist on both sides.

I don't remember if I felt any kind of inconvenience at that time. But by afternoon, I felt some stiffness over my shoulders. In the evening, we offered some prayers and burst a few crackers, as it was a small festival after Deepavali, an Indian festival of lights and crackers.

After that, I felt both my arms were locked. I just couldn't lift them beyond my waist. There was excruciating pain too. I took some painkillers that night but could not sleep properly due to the pain. The next day, that is on the 12th of November, I visited an orthopaedic surgeon. When the pain did not subside on the 13th also, I cancelled my ticket to London and back, which was from 15th to 21st November.

I later went to a neuro-surgeon who said a few nerves in the neck seemed to have got inflamed from what he called the 'barber's manipulation.' He suggested rest and some medicines. After I narrated to him the details of my cancelled trip and asked when I could plan to go, he said I could go any time but should put on a neck collar during journeys. He also joked that the moment I saw my daughter on landing at London, my pain would go away.

Encouraged by his advise, I left for London on 29th November and ended up with another traumatic experience there, a few days later, this time, a different one altogether.

Now, if the incident in India on the 11th of November was a forewarning for what lay in store for me in London, I did not or could not recognise it. I didn't see it that way in the first place. It did occur to me differently, more positively, that probably something major was averted by this incident. And it happened because I had to cancel my ticket to prevent something worse from happening in London. So I felt that the worst was over and everything was going to be great whenever I went.

But after the incident in London, when I was recollecting all that happened in my life in the recent past leading to the incident, I did not know how to relate it to my barber's experience back in India.

I was also wondering and still wonder whether the first incident in India was a forewarning for what lay in store in London. It also occurred to me that maybe a very major incident or accident had been averted with these two smaller events in quick succession. Probably, the major incident or accident got broken into two smaller ones and rescued me.

I can't stop smiling after writing this sentence. *Absolutely absurd!* I think. This is laughable. One can stretch one's imagination to any extent.

So, I resolve to conclude that, for mere mortals like me, there is no way one can foresee such accidents or incidents happening in life. However, can certain trauma-causing incidents or accidents be prevented by following some rules? There could be two simple rules:

One: Never risk attempting anything likely to even remotely cause a physical or psychological disturbance in our lives.

But that would be a boring life. No risk. No adventure. Just cautioning oneself all the time that some terrible experience might happen. That's absurd. But then, it is better than facing a traumatising one, even if it happens once in a hundred times. It's the individual's choice.

Two: If you have a chance to weigh whether to get involved in any experience or not, just see if the trauma such an experience would cause in the event of its failure outweighs the pleasure we get out of its success. Such experiences are also best avoided.

Read it again.

Let me see retrospectively what I did and should have done before getting into both the experiences that I experienced in November and December 2018.

The barber's manipulation: The pleasure I got from the twisting is far lesser than the pain that the experience caused me in the aftermath. Such experiences in our life, which gives more trauma when they fail than the pleasure they give if they succeed should best be avoided. It is only later I read that certain people have had permanent damage due to the so-called 'barber's manipulation.'

The juggler's deceit at Westminster's Bridge: It is a pure gamble, which is best avoided as seen by the above pleasure-pain rule. In the sense that, if it was only £10, then success is getting a profit of another £10, while failure is losing only £10. That is still ok. But as the stakes go high, the pleasure-pain equation reverses. So, even if I entered it, I should have put at stake only that much money which, whether I lost or won, could only be seen as some adventurous fun and nothing more than that. Instead, I allowed myself to get into a disastrous psychic trap, totally unprepared and unknown in my life.

REITERATION – STAGE I

READING THE WARNINGS BEFORE OCCURRENCE OF ANY TRAUMATIC EXPERIENCE.

FEAR OF FAILURES MAY NOT BE THE RIGHT WAY OUT

It is probably a stupid idea to live a life fearing all the time that something might go wrong every time we do something new or do something that did not work out well sometime in the past.

NOT ATTEMPTING ANYTHING DUE TO PAST FAILURES IS NOT A SOLUTION

If something failed in the past, expecting that it might fail again is foolish. But doing it in the same way as done earlier is even sillier because the chances of its failing are high. Try in a different way, more prepared, more cautiously so that chances of success are more.

WEIGHING SUCCESS AND FAILURE COULD POSSIBLY AVOID TRAUMA

If experiencing anything new, unprepared, for the first time, better weigh the outcome of success and failure. Every experience gives us pleasure or pain, depending on if it has succeeded or failed as per our expectations. And any experience likely to give more pain, if it fails, than pleasure if it succeeds is best avoided.

SECOND STAGE

RECOGNISING THE WARNING SIGNS DURING A TRAUMATIC INCIDENT AND WITHDRAWING BEFORE IT IS TOO LATE

Is there a way to read the warnings midway and pull out from a potentially traumatic experience before it is too late?

Walking into such experiences generally happens accidentally, maybe once or very few times in our lifetime. But their effect stays with us for a very long time, sometimes lifelong, depending on the intensity of its effect on our minds.

Why do we get there in the first place? I mean, why do we land ourselves in situations that are likely to put us in some precarious positions later? If at all we knew the answers to this question, we would never be confused whether we should get in there or not. One thing that can be said about these experiences is that, in most of these cases, we get in because *we are either curious to know how the experience would be or hope that the experience would be just a little fun with a happy ending.*

Curiosity. Curiosity about what? To experience the "fear of the unknown" with the hope that the "unknown" experience would be a pleasant one. The basic tendency of the human mind is to get itself into the unknown territory and experience the equally unknown outcome. And the "fear of the unknown" gives a great deal of adrenaline push. This entire process of excitement that we experience is probably what we call "an adventure." And we love adventures, don't we?

But when we plan an adventure, we train our mind and body to face it, and it generally leaves an exciting and fun-filled experience. But those that happen accidentally or that we have not prepared ourselves physically or mentally for, more often than not, lands us in an experience of "misadventure" or, sometimes, into a disaster.

Even in such an accidental "misadventure," something must be going on in our minds just before we let ourselves into such situations, where we are likely to experience unpleasantness immediately after.

Though we come face to face with such situations all of a sudden, what are the thoughts that occur in our mind when we are just about to enter them? How does the mind work and push us into a trap from where we find it difficult to wriggle out? Is there a way to get away from such situations either at the beginning or at some time not too late after we get ourselves into them? Let's see.

When we are suddenly exposed to a new unknown experience, our mind goes through various steps of responses—about three. One, of confusion, second, of acceptance, and then the third, the submission. And they occur in quick succession one after the other, not allowing us enough time into any of those steps. Let us discuss these three steps of responses:

THE THREE STEPS OF RESPONSES

First Step: State of Confusion: There is always a 'curiosity' element in our mind when something new is likely to happen in our life. This 'curiosity' element of the mind always wants to explore new, unexplored territory. There is not much of a problem when such events give us time to experience them. There is enough time to analyse between the curiosity in mind and our actions to experience them. This time that we get, between the curious phase and exploration phase, is the confusion phase. In a planned adventure, this confusion phase gets time to analyse and train to get into the exploration phase.

The problem is when they occur all of a sudden. In such situations, there is less time between the curious phase of the mind and the exploration phase. And hence, the time that the *mind remains in a confused state* is very less.

In this short time frame, the confused mind either jumps out of the situation or into it. **Whatever decision one has to take, it has to be in this short timeframe, which lasts a few moments only.** If due to some external factors (like someone cautioning us and forcing us out of it or we recollecting a similar experience of self or others), one is able to jump out of it, they would be lucky.

Left to the mind, the confused mind will only take us further into it, for that's how it is made to function. To explore new experiences. To experience "fear of the unknown," not allowing one to look into the consequences. Because the "fear of the unknown" itself causes an excitement, an adrenaline push, which we so much desire most of the time.

Is there any rule or mantra to check this? How does one know how to get out of it in those few seconds of "confusion"?

The answer lies there. In the word "confusion" itself. Whenever our mind is "confused" even for a second about getting into a particular situation, we should make it a rule not to get involved. The reason is very simple.

If we come out of such experiences feeling excited and pleasurable, the intensity of the positive impact on us is much less when compared to the intensity of the negative impact on us if it turns out to be a misadventure or a disaster.

It means such sudden experiences, where our mind is confused about whether to enter or not, are best left not experiencing. Because if, in the end, it turns out to be a disastrous experience, the impact on us is far more intense and painful than the pleasure we get when it is a successful experience. The very state of confusion is because of that.

Second Step: State of Acceptance: Now, let us say, due to reasons beyond our control, we landed on the second step after facing such sudden situations. That is we have entered it and are in the process of experiencing it. Here again, there will be a time when we will halt for a second or two and hesitate if we continue. That is the last warning to us, and one should pull out of such situations even if we are halfway through it.

That few seconds of hesitation is a warning by something in us telling us to withdraw. And if we fail to withdraw, there are no more warnings. We are deep into it and have to undergo the experience. And we will be automatically pushed into the third step.

Third Step: State of Submission: We have now entered a point of no return in our experiencing some event in our life that we have almost no control of until something jolts us. But by then, it has already made a disastrous and shocking impact on us. So, even if we realise our mistake, there is no way to mend it, as the damage is already done. All we can do is to be a witness to the experience and stay numb with shock until the pain actually starts seeping into our system, and we gradually start to feel it.

And now, we can start blaming someone saying we have been "psyched," "tricked" or/and "deceived." "Deceived" by someone, something, fate, luck, situation, time, etc. And when we run out of options, God, if you believe in one, is always there to be blamed. We can apportion blame on anyone or anything that comes to our mind because we refuse to accept one thing.

That we have been "tricked" by none other than our own mind.

Mind, which is on the lookout for new adventures.

Mind, which succumbed to experiencing the unknown without preparation.

Mind, which is not in our own control.

Mind, which is running our lives and not the other way round.

Mind, which is our own but gets trapped in someone else's control.

Situations and events in our lives are what they are. People are what they are. People do what they do. Time is what it is. None of these interferes with our lives until and unless we draw them towards us, through an instrument. That instrument is none other than our own "mind." And then we experience all these through our mind the way it dictates us. It dictates our actions. It dictates our emotions. It even dictates the outcomes.

A closer look at the three steps, of confusion, Acceptance and submission, in every situation, shows how our own mind plays havoc with us.

Let's see this in more detail through a small story.

Just before I started to write this section of the book, I came across a short one-minute video clip on WhatsApp. A very traumatic experience of a man who didn't live to experience the consequence himself but his dear ones, who were filming it, had to live with this experience throughout their lives.

A person was being filmed looking at an elephant some 100 yards away grazing in a field. Voices of men, women and children were heard from behind the video being taken on a mobile.

The person who was being filmed was moving towards the elephant, wanting to be filmed along with the elephant from close quarters.

He was slowly running towards the elephant shouting at it with a raised arm. When he was about 80 yards from the elephant, it looked at him from there and, as a warning, moved its head sideways, as though saying, "No, no, no. You dare not come near me."

The person was in no mood to understand the warning and went closer. Seeing him getting closer to her, the elephant also turned and moved towards him. Both were running slowly towards each other.

When he was about 30 yards away, he hesitated for a second, looked behind towards the camera, laughed and moved towards her again, slowly though. Now, people behind were getting worried, and a woman's voice shouted at him to come back.

He stopped for a few seconds and started waving at the elephants again, shouting something. The elephant had decided not to take the attack lightly and was still moving towards him.

When the elephant was as close as ten feet away, he stopped, still waving his hand, saying something loudly. The elephant was in no mood to stop and came charging.

By the time he realised that he should backtrack, it was already very close to him. It pushed him down with its trunk, and in full view of his people filming the scene, she crushed his head with its foreleg. A ghastly scene.

His people ran towards the elephant, shouting at it to move away. But then it was too late. He was wriggling in pain and seemed to be taking his last breath. He must have died by the time his people reached him. And the elephant was seen going back into the forest through the fields.

All this happened in just a minute or so.

Now, here is where the cautions and warnings were.

Firstly, it is absolutely foolish to have ventured into such an adventure, knowing very well that it was a wild elephant. Even if it was not, going near it without its mahout is foolhardy.

This is the first word of caution: never to venture near an unknown adventure without prior knowledge or training.

If at all we have to move into the second phase, let's see where the three steps are applicable.

The first step of confusion in the mind occurred when he was about 60 feet away and stopped for a brief moment. Without any second thought, seeing the charging elephant, he should just run back. But the "fear of the unknown" adventurous mind played its mischief. It made him ignore his own confused state as well as warnings from his people behind. The adrenaline push caused him to take further steps, only in the wrong direction.

The second step of acceptance came when he was just about 10 feet away from the elephant, which was not heeding to his shouting and gestures. Here, he was getting the last warning after he had decided to accept and face the experience. That brief second or two was his last chance, if at all he had any, in this particular circumstance, to back off and run back for his life. That split-second hesitation when death was staring at his face would have saved his life. But then something (his own mind) pushed him further. And then,

The third and last stage of submission was the point of no return when the elephant pushed him down with its trunk and stamped on him. That was THE END of his life.

This incident in his life was where the third and last stage of submission (to the experience) was *literally* *'a point of no return' for him.* But in most cases, we live with the traumatic experience for the rest of our lives not knowing how to deal with it. Now, his people will have to live with this experience, which is a traumatising experience for them.

Let us check my experience. In my case, the three steps can be explained as follows:

The first step of confusion (to enter into the experience) occurred when I was showing the scene to my daughter, I took out a twenty-pound note and stopped for a while wondering if I should venture into the experience or not. But the excitement of a possible fun-filled adventure from the "fear of the unknown" of an adventurous mind played its mischief. It made me ignore my own confused state as well as my reluctant daughter's. The adrenaline push made me take further steps towards the man. And I landed myself into experiencing the unknown.

*The Second S*tep of Acceptance (of the experience) came when I stopped for a few seconds after already shelling out a few fifty-pound notes to the man. During those few seconds, I got a bit suspicious about the fellow who was continuously shouting in my ears with the most exasperating voice. So that was the last warning I got to take back the money and retreat. But then, I had already 'accepted' that I would experience the event and had deliberately decided to ignore the subtle warning. And I let go an unbelievable amount of fifty-pound notes in just a few minutes, just like that.

The third and last step of submission (to the experience of a lifetime) was when I surrendered to the situation and let go of a few more tens and twenty-pound notes at the instance of the two girls and myself also feeling confident (more out of desperation) that by winning this round, I could get back what I lost. This (false) sense of hope to salvage whatever little I could was like a desperate attempt to avoid drowning by holding on to a straw." I drowned nevertheless.

Something in us gives a warning minutes before we venture into some unknown, speculative, possibly adventurous experience of our life. More often than not, we ignore it. No, override it. Thanks to our mind and its control over us.

Now, let me highlight the warnings we should never ignore:

1. *Any situation and experience that one is facing for the first time or after a long time and is likely to cause **more agony if it fails than the pleasure it gives if it is a success** is best discarded straight away. The best way to discard it is to turn away from it.*

2. *Just before getting into such situations, while the mind is drawing us into it, something in us stops us for a moment from entering it—**momentary fear, or momentary distraction, or a simple warning from someone dear to us, or just a simple impulsive back step**. These are enough to be read as warnings and move away from it. Mind you, no egos here.*

3. *If one still gets into it, ignoring all the cautions, one more such momentary caution occurs while one is in the middle of such situations. These are even more difficult to read, but if one is able to see it, this is the last chance to get away from them, even if it is midway and half the damage is already done.*

4. *There is no warning beyond this. It is only experiencing and, in most cases, suffering the consequences.*

> *How do we tackle the consequences, this suffering which occurs due to the misadventure that we got ourselves into? Now, that is a very important issue.*

Let us deal with it now.

REITERATION – SECOND STAGE

READING THE WARNINGS MIDWAY AND PULLING OUT FROM A POTENTIALLY TRAUMATIC EXPERIENCE BEFORE IT'S TOO LATE

STATE OF CONFUSION

Just before we try to get into a situation with a confused mind, they are best avoided. Confusion occurs because we are unsure. Confusion occurs because, if it fails, we know the outcome would be traumatic. Confusion occurs simply because we are not prepared for it. Mostly, unprepared events end up as failures.

MID-COURSE CORRECTION

It is possible to read certain warnings in the middle of such experiences. That is, if there is some sanity still left in the mind. The mind would lookout for an escape route for a brief period, maybe lasting a few seconds. It would look for suggestion, hints, help or a way out. And it can come from anywhere—from near and dear ones, a flash of sudden fear, or sometimes from unexpected quarters. If we heed, we will pass. If not, stay and be doomed.

THIRD STAGE

DEALING WITH THE TRAUMA CAUSED BY THE EXPERIENCE

Once experienced, what is the way to transform a regretful and unforgettable outcome of a traumatic experience into a powerful and positive one?

This is the section I wanted to write this book for, for obvious reasons. I have already experienced the event and am now facing the aftermath.

In the first two sections, I attempted to give readers the possibility of reading any warnings and see if one could pull out at various stages of such experiences.

More often than not, we can neither predict the happenings of such experiences in our lives nor can we prevent them just before they are likely to happen. That is because none of us wants to live our lives doubting or being cautious of every experience as a negative one.

Once we have gone through it, the trauma caused by such an experience stays with us for a long time, maybe lifelong. They bother us day in day out. The initial days after the incident are more difficult to bear than the days later. Numerous thoughts occur immediately after the event. They are the last thoughts that occur at night before sleeping. And again, they are the first ones to occur when one gets up in the morning. *Tsunami* or *bombardment of thoughts* is the right term.

What kind of thoughts? Well, these were a few that occurred in my case:

The deceit. How could I be deceived?

How did I allow myself to be tricked?

How could some stranger psyche me like this?

How did I fall into the trap?

Why the hell did it happen in the first place?

How could I not read the warnings?

Where exactly did I go wrong?

Did I deserve it?

Whatever happened to all my prayers and good deeds?

It goes on and on and on…

As the days roll by, the frequency of such thoughts is reduced, but they occur nevertheless. Whenever a situation, even remotely connected with the incident appears, the experience is replayed. The same shock and shame is experienced, even if it is for a moment. But it does. And one knows, it will never go.

But it has to go. One cannot carry on like that. It invades every activity of life. It undermines our confidence. Our self-esteem. And that is too bad. It cannot be allowed to do that. More so, when one feels it is not their fault. And even if one feels that it is their fault, what has already happened should not dictate one's present and future life.

Now, the thoughts of how to overcome the trauma the experience had caused were bothering me more than the trauma itself. How to live with that experience was the actual problem. Only those who have had such an experience can imagine the tsunami of thoughts that came from all directions.

Finally, I did come up with something that looked like a solution.

When it occurred to me first, I mean the solution, I was so excited that I felt suddenly enlightened. I had a beaming smile on my face for a long time. For the first time after the experience, I was at ease with myself. The very thought that I could find a solution to this mental menace in itself brought about a positive transformation in me. Luckily for me, this happened barely one week after the incident.

The 'solution' will have to wait. I want to bring out something else before that. About such traumatic events and how they affect us.

TRAUMATIC EVENTS AND THEIR EFFECTS ON US

From the ownership point of view, we would want to hold at least two people to blame for the situations we land ourselves in, particularly nasty ones. Invariably most of the time we feel that some other person or persons are responsible for it. And when there is no such other person in the vicinity, we hold HIM responsible for what happened. Very rarely, do we accept that most of the times, it is because of our own selves that we land in such irrevocable traumatic situations.

However much we would like to deny, in reality, it is we who are responsible for putting ourselves through such traumatic experiences. Of course, other people appear to cause it to us. But they only act as instruments or catalysts. They are the medium. We are the culprits. Actual culprits. But we are in constant denial of this and constantly in search of a scapegoat. This, obviously, is to calm our egos. Of course, it does help us to some extent but only temporarily, and we will never be able to find a solution this way because the problem lies somewhere else. I mean, not 'somewhere else' literally. But right here. In us. Within ourselves.

In tackling this fellow, who is our own self, lies the solution. And this "fellow" in us needs to be tackled before, during and after such experiences. There are no warnings of such events, before or when they occur.

Even if there is, we do not know how to be aware or recognise them. So that leaves us with no choice but to know how to tackle the effects of such traumatic experiences after they have occurred.

Before the remedy is discussed, we need to see where the damages or traumas occur in us on experiencing such events. That is, which parts of us get affected by such trauma.

From the point of awareness about ourselves as human beings, there are three aspects or areas or realms under which we operate:

1. Body

2. Mind and

3. Soul

Of these, we have been told that the "soul" is indestructible, undamageable and unaffected by external or any kind of disturbances. We have also been told that the "soul" is above the other two, mind and body. If we go deeper into this subject, we will delve into spirituality, which is not my goal. We need to discuss this at a more material level because that is where this physical world that we live in keeps us.

So that leaves us with the *body* and *mind* through which we operate our material life. Now, these two are the actual victims that get affected by traumatic experiences. They are the ones that suffer the consequences of such experiences. They are the ones that carry the scars of such happenings. They are the ones who keep reminding "us" of the traumatic experience. In fact, they are the ones who are experiencing it. Finally, "they" are the ones that "we" identify "ourselves" with. And since we identify ourselves with these two, we need to find a solution within these two.

Of these, the body carries the physical wounds, if any, from traumatic experiences. And over time, the wounds heal. There may be scars left, but the pain from the wound may go. There might be even permanent disability from some experiences, but one gets used to that also. Sometimes, their life might come to an end, which relieves them from any trauma thereafter. But then, that in itself is a traumatic experience for their near and dear ones.

Thus, the main sufferer is our mind. Or can we say, "we" suffer because of our mind? Do not worry if you are confused about what I have just said. Believe me, even I was equally confused. The question is, who is this 'we' and who is this 'mind'? Are they different, or are they the same?

Well, in this material and physical world of experiences, they are the same. That is because we constantly identify ourselves as our mind perceives us. But then the next question is, how does our mind perceive us? It does not perceive 'us.' It just perceives. That's all. It accumulates. It stores. It reminds. It analyses. It makes judgements. It concludes. It confuses. It makes the body react. Through emotions. Through actions. Through reactions. Through experiences, again.

And then. It stores again. It analyses. It makes judgements. It concludes. It confuses through experiences, again. And again.

The cycle goes on. The suffering goes on. The joys too go on. But sufferings have very strong bearings.

The emotions from negative experiences are stronger than the emotions from positive experiences. Moreover, emotions of negative experiences play themselves again and again in the mind. This makes the sufferings from negative experiences stronger than the pleasure we get from positive experiences. And that's why negative experiences are difficult to tackle.

THE MIND AND ITS CONTROL OVER US

Now, the question is how to tackle this mind, which appears to have a stronger affinity to negativity than positivity. It rewinds and plays negative experiences again and again, over and over, more than positive experiences. The problem is that most of us do not know how to tackle it. Why I said most of us is because there are a few people, the spiritually inclined ones, who have managed to tame their minds. For them, experiences, good or bad, joyful or traumatic, mean nothing. They can manage to see every experience in the same light. Embrace spirituality if you want to reach there.

But the majority of us are stuck deep in the tornados of our minds. And tackling this tornado through the material realm is extremely difficult. For this, we need to delve some more into this element of our existential experience called the 'mind.'

We are constantly struggling between two facets of our mind. In other words, all our actions are guided by two aspects of our mind. One part, the basic instinctive one, is what we are and the other, the ideal part, is what we want to be.

Our life is a continuous battle between these two aspects of the mind. The 'basic' and the 'ideal' mind. And the 'via media' we come out with for every experience defines what we are. We identify ourselves with this 'via media' condition of the mind. Our sufferings, our happiness, all our emotions are an outcome of these aspects through which we live and operate.

The basic instinctive nature of the mind is to always seek gratification or pleasure. It will try to drive us towards experiencing that kind of life where we get or are likely to get immediate pleasures and which does not bother about the consequences. Our basic tendencies are to please our senses, come what may. We crave for that right after the time we are born, till we realise or at least are made to realise the dos and don'ts and rights and wrongs of our thoughts and actions. That is primarily because the instant we are born, our connection with the outer world is only through the functions of our five senses—the auditory, visual, tactile, gustatory and olfactory.

While this is one part of the mind, there is this other part, which is the "ideal one." Or wanting to be "ideal one." The one that shows the 'right way.' The ethical way, moral way—the way humans in their ideal form ought to think, behave and act. The way one would be liked, appreciated and exemplified. The one that places us above other living beings, so we think. The one that appears and is established after we have known how to deliberate and discriminate our thoughts, actions and behaviours. The one that we have been taught or we ourselves have learned during growing stages of our life.

Our struggle throughout life has been to strike a balance between these two facets of the mind. One is natural, which we have right from the time we are born until we die. The other is acquired during our journey of life, through learning from various sources. These sources could be social norms, cultures, traditions, religions, elders, scriptures, laws and also our own experiences.

We are not born with an instinctive nature of the mind. By itself, the mind is the purest and the most powerful part of us human beings. It is this, which makes or breaks us. The moment we are born into this material world, the senses are exposed to all material things around us. And senses need gratification. Eyes see and want what they see. The ears hear and want what they hear. The nose smells and wants what it smells. The tongue tastes and wants what it tastes. Touch feels and wants what it feels. The auditory, visual, tactile, gustatory and olfactory functions of our five senses, namely mouth, eyes, touch, tongue and nose, are so powerful that throughout our lives, we are driven by them. It is as though our existence is only to satisfy them. Thus, the basic nature or instinctive part of the mind is formed here, immediately after our birth. And it remains so throughout our lives unless and until reined in by the self or an external force.

THE BASIC INSTINCTIVE MIND VS. THE IDEAL MIND

The sensory aspect of the mind, the basic nature or instinct gratification part, will always pop up first in the everyday experiential arena in our life. Then the struggle of applying that other 'ideal' part of the mind defines the outcome of the experience, depending on when it has been applied—before, during or after the experience.

When this ideal mind wakes up after we have already gone through an experience, particularly an unpleasant one, we are left with a battered conscience and a tormented mind. If it is applied before or while experiencing it, one might still salvage oneself from the turmoil of a troubled mind. When and how this 'ideal' part of the mind is applied in day-to-day life's experience depends on how strongly one has been able to establish it in one's own being. And that depends upon how well one has developed a strong will to deliberate and discriminate one's own actions.

The application of the 'ideal' mind also depends on how strongly the 'basic' mind is ruling our life. When this 'basic' mind is shrouded or engulfed with a strong desire, sometimes-unrealistic ones, the implementation of the 'ideal' mind is very difficult until that desire is satiated. The stronger the desire, the harder it is to overcome the 'basic' instinctive nature of the mind. And if the desire is not satiated, it is further engulfed by emotions like irritations, frustrations or anger. And now it becomes even more difficult to overcome the basic mind's craving for instant gratification. And one gets deeper into the trap until one is doomed. Doom could be anything from pushing oneself to guilt, depression, mindlessness or even extreme steps like taking one's own or others' lives.

WHY DO WE GET INTO EXPERIENCES?

The first thing that comes up just before we experience any situation is our senses. We can say that they (our senses) are the reason we drive ourselves into any situations.

The auditory, visual, tactile, gustatory and olfactory functions of our five senses, namely, mouth, eyes, touch, tongue and nose, are so powerful that we, by our very nature, are drawn to satiate them through the mind. Satiating means we crave for the emotions or feelings that arise from satisfying these senses. Like the thrilling sensations we feel, pleasurable feelings, excitement, a (many a time, false) sense of achievement, satisfaction, and such temporary fulfilment of the cause of our existence. In other words, our basic (or natural) desire to appease our senses is the reason why we get into any experience in our life's journey. After the experience is over, we hope to 'enjoy' the effects of such appeasement.

THE SENSES AND THE OUTCOME OF THEIR APPEASEMENT

What we need to understand is that, if senses are appeased, there is a (false) sense of achievement and (a short-lived) satisfaction. But if not, the negative emotions drive us to lust for it again. In both cases, appeasement or no appeasement, we drive ourselves into such experiences again and again. In the first case, after they are appeased, we look for newer or similar experiences again. And in the second case, if not appeased, we look for similar or newer ones again until appeasement is achieved. However, in the first case where the senses are appeased, we are at least in a positive frame of mind, albeit for a short period. But in the second case where the senses are not appeased, the negative emotions drive us crazy.

THE OUTCOME OF NEGATIVE EMOTIONS

Why some experiences drive us crazy is because we forget or tend to overlook the fact that the outcomes of experiences may not always be pleasant or may not always result in a sense of fulfilment. Sometimes, the outcomes are disastrous. They cause pain, disappointment, dissatisfaction, irritation, anger, frustrations, and such negative emotions and feelings that are hard to overcome. This further makes us lust for the sensory gratification we missed in the earlier instances.

THE ALIENATION OF THE 'IDEAL' MIND

By now, this lust for sensory gratification becomes so strong that all the negative emotions accumulated shrouds or engulfs the basic instinctive mind in such a manner that it is shut off from any input from the ideal mind, the mind that can navigate us away from the negative impact of experiences.

In such situations, the curtains or clouds of negative emotions become so powerful that they totally alienate the ideal mind of even the most learned person, who then becomes helpless and powerless against the force of the basic instinctive mind. One is now trapped in the basic instinctive mind's only ways, and that is the desire to satiate or appease the senses. Until, of course, one is faced with doom. And the doom could be anything from sadness, depression, insanity, mindlessness, tendencies to takes lives, etc.

REIGNING IN THE BASIC INSTINCTIVE MIND

Hence, the catch is, when should the ideal mind take control or at what stage should the basic instinctive mind be reined in? Also, how does one recover from doom, once fallen into the trap, and pull oneself out of such situations?

To reign in the basic instinctive mind, one should have very strongly established the ideal mind in one's own life. How and when we succumb to the instinctive mind depends on how much we have in-grilled into our daily existential lives the contents of the ideal mind like ethics, morals, values, etc.

Those whose lives are completely governed by the learnings of the 'ideal' mind can always manage to reign in their senses or the longings of the basic instinctive mind at all times. They do not allow the senses to take control of any situation. They are the blessed ones. Trained and spiritual ones. But such people are rare.

Those whose lives are never governed by the learnings of the 'ideal' mind always succumb to the cravings of the basic instinctive mind and suffer between pleasure and pain. Both pleasure and pain here are sufferings because the mind is always restless to gain access to one and deny access to the other. They will go to any extent to achieve these accesses. They do not believe in living with ethics or morals or any principles. They live in a world created by their own egocentric and self-proclaimed identity. They are the ones with eccentric, at times, dangerous minds. Such people are also few.

Those who have enough knowledge of the contents of the 'ideal' mind, but take time to put them into practice, are the ones who constantly struggle with reigning in the desires of the basic instinctive mind. When they succumb to the instinctive mind, they subsequently get entrapped by such emotions as guilt, regret, self-accusations, blameworthiness, conscience battering, revengefulness, et cetera. Most people are, of course, in this category.

It would be interesting, I thought, to represent this pictorially. Let us assume that our thoughts, behaviour and actions are engulfed in a circle whose boundary represents the influence of the state of our mind, ideal or basic instinctive nature, on them. The three states discussed above can be depicted as follows:

1. ***Engulfed only by the ideal mind (that is, the basic instinctive mind is fully under control):***

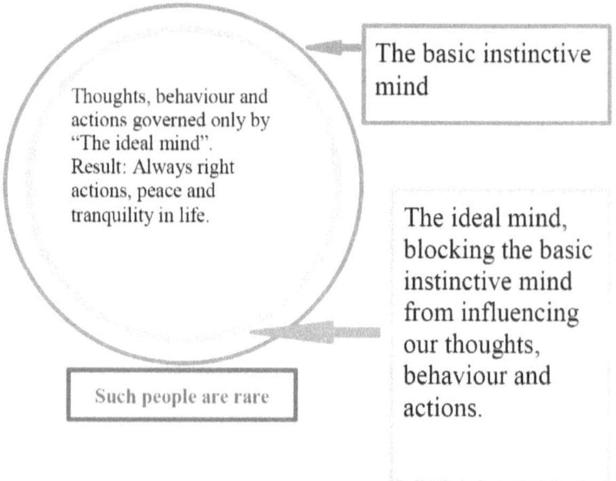

2. ***Engulfed only by the basic instinctive mind (that is, the ideal mind lies dormant):***

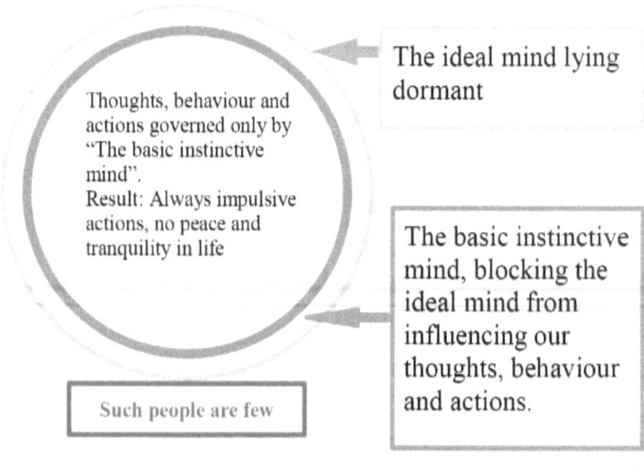

3. ***Both the basic instinctive mind and the ideal mind struggle to play predominance:***

> Both the basic instinctive mind and the ideal mind keep influencing our thoughts, behaviour and actions, depending on which is predominant at that point in time.

THE EGO HASSLE

Is there anything else we need to know that drives our life? Other than the mind?

Yes! Emotions and ego, perhaps.

Here again, there are positive and negative emotions. Positive emotions are joy, happiness, pleasantness, confidence, courage, calmness, etc. Negative emotions are sadness, anger, frustrations, irritations, depression, and the like. Positive emotions give us energy; negative emotions drain us of energy.

Most of the time, when our ego is satisfied, we get positive emotions. And when our ego is hurt, we land up with negative emotions. Does that mean that our mind is egocentric? Mind with ego is negative emotions. Mind with ego-lessness is positive emotions. And where does this ego live? Where does it exist? In the mind? Yes, it does reside there. So can we say that ego is another entity operating within the mind? Sometimes, maybe operating the mind itself. And then, in turn, us.

Here we are. Another term. Another realm through which we operate in the material world. 'Ego.' This ego we are talking about is the one that is more inclined towards the 'basic' instinctive nature of the mind.

So what do we have here? **Body, mind, emotions and ego**. All interconnected. If not complementing, at least supplementing each other.

Emotions, though a bi-product, we just cannot ignore them, as they are the outcome, a visible outcome of the interactions between the other three.

Finally, does this mean that we identify ourselves with this ego? Now, what is this ego? We need to delve into it in more detail.

Ego is the reason we act the way we act in our life. It is part of the mind, in the mind, sometimes the mind itself. It is not only the cause of our actions but also the effect of it. We behave the way we behave because of ego. It is that part of the mind that forces us to be in a certain way. Dealing with it is the trickiest part of our life. It is also that part of the mind, which tries to draw a balance between the basic instinctive mind and the ideal one. Hasn't our life's struggle always been to draw a balance between our basic instinctive nature of the mind and the ideal way it should be?

Now, this via media, the ego, always strives for a balance between the other two, the 'instinctive' and the 'ideal.' Meaning, it tends to satisfy both the 'instinctive' mind as well as the 'ideal' one. This is the mind that we identify ourselves with. And this 'ego' behaves differently in different situations.

Our basic instinctive mind pops up first in every situation we are faced with. That is, the gratification of the five senses, either one or more, is the basic nature of the mind in every situation. And then, this ego, our identity, is 'hurt' when the mind's basic instincts are not satiated. The ideal part can calm it down, depending on how strongly one has been able to imbibe it in one's own self or being. However, a certain portion of our basic instincts needs to be satisfied if one has to exist.

Hence, some of our ego needs to be satiated. That part that does not cause harm either to self or others while it is being satiated. And since it is trying to draw a balance between the basic and the ideal mind and, more so, since we identify ourselves with it, keeping it in good spirits makes sense.

Satisfying this harmless ego, without doubt, is essential. We pacify this; our emotions change. We please this ego; the storm in our mind gets mitigated. Something in us makes us feel better. The traumatic experience changes into something more bearable, albeit for a short while. Of course, it is for a short while, because the basic instinctive ego-mind is made like that. No permanent solution there. Nevertheless, it has to be satiated. Because that is the biggest block that hinders us from thinking rationally, stably, calmly. It blocks even the ideal mind from playing its part in our life.

The 'ideal' ego-mind also needs to be satisfied because, ultimately, it is that portion of the mind that gives us lasting joy and happiness.

IS THERE A SOLUTION TO A TROUBLED MIND?

By solution, I mean, a way out. Is there a way to subdue the troubled mind and mitigate its negative effects on us? There is, of course, one way, which is sulk over it and feel victimised all the time. *This way, one can rest assured that they would never be able to get over it. This, which most people resort to, acts only as a catalyst to further the trauma, not mitigate it. Hence, I am not even terming it as a way to deal with it.*

However, there two other ways to deal with such a situation. One, although it mitigates the effect, is not a positive approach because it primarily aims at satisfying the basic instinctive mind and the ego. I will term it as **solution by negative means**. The other way is a more powerful one as it involves dealing with one's own self by transforming in a more positive way. Hence, I shall call it **solution by positive means**.

Now, let us see them in detail.

Solution by Negative Means

By negative means, I mean 'revenge.' Give back to the person or persons who have caused us this trauma or have put us in a situation that caused us the damage. And when we cannot do that, cause harm to one's own self.

We must have observed that every time something bad happens to us, we are in search of someone to blame—some scapegoat. And when we don't find anyone to blame, we are constantly looking to blame that invisible someone (we don't even spare God, at times) for putting us in such situations. This defensive mechanism saves us from further damaging the already bruised ego.

And if that someone is known to us or within our reach, we would love to cause similar damage to that person(s). *Revenge.* It gives us immense satisfaction or, rather, satisfies our ego to a very large extent. It gives us some kind of pleasure, though sadistic in nature. Further, we call this revenge as punishment when someone has deliberately caused us harm that we cannot forget. And when it is not caused deliberately, this revenge is in the form of "letting someone know how much pain they have caused us." That's why they say, "Revenge, sweet revenge." But is it? I doubt that.

Ultimately, deep down, it does leave us with a feeling—we may call it guilt—that we have behaved exactly in the same manner that the other person has behaved with us. In that, how are we different from them?

This type of solution to get over our experiences, the revenge type, is definitely not a lasting solution. I mean, it might give us relief but definitely not leave a positive impact on our lives. Nor does it set an example for others who are facing such situations to follow.

Now here, there is one thing I should elucidate. Let us not confuse ourselves with a legal course of action against someone for any wrongdoing, when and if required. It is, of course, required by all means. My point is that taking the law in our hands by punishing someone ourselves might not serve the purpose in a positive way.

SOLUTION BY POSITIVE MEANS

But is there a way out? YES, THERE IS! A solution that would not only pull us out of such a traumatic experience but also lets us feel proud about the way we have dealt with it. What's more, it is the best way out for anyone who has been subjected to such situations to follow. And that is to deal with it positively.

How to positively deal with an uncomfortable, inexplicable, unwanted, haunting and traumatic experience?

It is simply by accepting what happened 'as it is' and coming out stronger than ever before. Easier said than done, right? But it is possible. There are numerous people whose lives were devastated by unimaginable traumatic experiences but have emerged as strong individuals to reckon with, for people to learn from and who have shown how to face the world boldly and triumphantly. Whether they have acted consciously or not is not known, but learn from them, we can.

But to learn how to accept what happened 'as it is' and come out of it more powerfully than ever before, **by making a conscious effort**, is my endeavour.

Before I arrive at that, let us see how a traumatised mind affects us.

Effect of a traumatising experience on us

We need to identify what, in the experience, has been affecting us most. We can do this by listing out at least a few of the thoughts that recur again and again. They could be anything from material losses like physical wellbeing, money and people to psychological effects like self-respect, ego, self-confidence and self-esteem. Then just categorise them into the two major groups—**material losses and psychological effects**. In the end, we will see that most of the effects can be brought under these two major heads, which when taken care of will ease our trauma for sure.

How I went about it is discussed below.

How to work this out?

Now, here is what we need to do. Identify the losses we had to endure due to the experience that can be termed as material losses. And also identify which part of the incident has a direct impact on our psyche. But how do we know which impacted to what extent? There must be a way. Maybe, by rating the impact on a scale of 0 to 10. '0' being no impact or has not recurred as thoughts and '10,' maximum impact or that which has kept recurring repeatedly in our mind.

In my case, this is how I rated my thoughts that kept recurring:

	Thoughts that kept crossing my mind	Affect on 'Mind'	Material/ Psychological
1	*The money I lost was huge, considering that during my entire stay, I did not intend to spend even 10% of what I threw away in a few minutes.*	10	Material
2	*The manner in which the guy could manage to psyche me.*	10	Psychological
3	*The thought, "How can I get back the money I lost?"*	10	Material

4	How I got fooled in front of my daughter or her friend.	7	Psychological
5	The thought that I had no control over myself.	**8**	Psychological
6	The thought that I wouldn't be able to discuss this with anyone else.	7	Psychological
7	The thought that what would my daughter and her friend think about me.	7	Psychological
8	The fear that this incident would leave a lasting negative effect on my life.	**9**	Psychological
9	What would anyone who gets to know of this incident think of me?	7	Psychological
10	The manner in which I succumbed to greed.	7	Psychological
11	The thought that why did this happen to me at all.	**6**	Psychological
12	The thought 'I should have never been there.'	**2**	Psychological
13	The thought 'Will I ever be able to just accept it?'	**8**	Psychological
14	*The determination that I have to overcome it.*	**10**	Psychological
15	*The thought that somehow I needed to bring it out into the open.*	**10**	Psychological
16	*The desire to somehow caution people and prepare them to tackle such incidents in life.*	**10**	Psychological

These are not the only thoughts that occurred in my mind. The mind is an extremely powerful matter in our body. It can manage to bring in hundreds and hundreds of thoughts, related or not, in just a minute. But those that impact us most are the ones which repeat themselves again and again for days, months, years or lifelong.

From the above analysis, I could see that just about two issues were bothering me, which could be called **material loss**. The rest were all more to do with an effect on my psyche.

Hence, the solution lay in addressing these two aspects—material and psychological effects, commensurate with their intensity of affect over us.

THE SOLUTION

THREE STEPS TO TRANSFORMING A TROUBLED MIND INTO A POSITIVE FORCE

STEP ONE: ACCEPT IT AS IT IS

The first step is to 'accept' and learn to 'live' with it. 'Accept' it as just an experience that has happened in this journey of our life. Easier said than done, right? But it has to be understood nice and clear that one cannot hide, override or erase any experience from our lives. Once they have happened, they are there to stay. Stay in our mind. The only way we can reduce the effect, particularly the negative effects of the unpleasant experience, is by saying, if possible loudly, to ourselves that 'what has happened has happened,' and nothing can be done about the way it happened. This self-declaration will help us reduce the turmoil in our mind. *That is, do not do any analysis of the hows, wheres, whys, whats, whens, etc. Stop being judgemental about the incident. Otherwise, there is a danger that this negativity will percolate into every other activity of our lives. And that will lower our self-confidence, self-esteem and self-respect.*

How did I handle my first step: I came to my senses as soon as the experience was over, and I overcame my initial shock. That could be because of a strong ethical sense, though it lit a bit late. Within a few minutes of my shock, I started telling myself to calm down and take it as it is. "It happened, and I got cheated. There is nothing I can do about it as of now." I found myself telling the girls too to take it as it is and keep calm. It was difficult for all three of us. I just told them to imagine a few days ahead, or few months ahead or maybe even a year or two ahead. As it is, the impact of this will be alleviated by then. It will give some solace today imagining that. It helped me. Within a few days, I found myself looking for a way to get over this in a positive and powerful manner.

SECOND STEP: MAKING GOOD THE MATERIAL LOSS, IF POSSIBLE

The money I lost was one of the first shocks I got from the incident. How I lost it only occurred later. This loss of money happened solely because of my curiosity and desire to experience something new as well as to make a quick buck. And both are the outcomes of my basic instinctive nature of mind. That nature of mind that is the first to exercise itself in any experience unless we have prepared or planned for it. Or unless we have developed a strong resolve to overcome it by our ideal mind.

The effect of the material loss will stay, maybe dormant in the mind, unless we make good of it, if we can. So making up that loss cannot be ignored and has to be attempted. If the attempt is honest and without malice towards anyone or anything, even if we do not make it up, the attempt itself will give solace. The very idea of attempting to make up the loss in itself will reduce the turmoil in the mind.

How did I attempt my second step?

Within days, four days precisely, I decided how to get back my money without causing harm to anyone and maybe by benefitting people. So when I first got the idea of writing about the incident, the first thing that came to my mind was "Well, if I publish this book, I might be able to make good at least some of the loss, if not more." And that really helped me in looking beyond the debilitating effect on my mind from the shock of losing my hard-earned money. Whether I really get something out of this is secondary, but the very idea transformed the agony in my mind into hope, which in itself is a positive energy.

THIRD STEP: TACKLING THE PSYCHOLOGICAL EFFECTS ON THE MIND

In the list of thoughts mentioned above, most of them are more psychological by nature than physical or materialistic. These thoughts were something to do with the way I expected myself to be, and I could not be. I failed to live up to my own expectations about myself as an ethically strong person who has his mind in his control. And second, I felt I failed to live up to how I hoped others perceived me. A mental situation where I had fallen in my own eyes. Wherein I feel that the so-called 'idealistic' learnings in my life have not been strong enough for me to overcome the powerful materialistic cravings or the basic instinctive nature of the mind. The recurring thoughts are the result of the conflict within, which is unable to accept or come to terms with the fact that I am not so resolute with my "idealistic" mindset. Now, that is a tough thing to live with.

These take some time to go away. Their effects are such that one's own personality takes a beating. One loses self-confidence, starts experience low self-esteem and doubts one's own ability to live an idealistic way of life. That "idealistic part of our mind," which one has established over a period of time through experience and knowledge, takes a battering.

How powerfully we have been able to transform this dimension of our traumatic mind will actually define our future life. Dealing with this in a powerful way would lift our drowning self-confidence and self-esteem. The action one takes to handle such a condition is what would transform the traumatising experience into a motivating one. This would help accept the experience itself as it is, without any anger, hatred or malice. What should such an action be?

SUCH ACTION IS….

Something big and powerful should be done. Something that would make the experience itself look small. That which would benefit a large section of the population. Like doing something for people who have faced similar situations. Maybe do something entirely different that would be a motivation for others. Basically, do something for the benefit of humanity.

How did I take my third step?

Within a few days of the experience, I got this idea of writing a book about it and help people understand the mind and ways to rein it in. The very idea gave me goosebumps. The trauma from the experience just started to meltdown, and in its place, ideas about how to go about it started taking shape. The slow transformation gave me an excitement that knew no bounds. That I may be able to make a difference to people's lives, particularly those who must have faced a similar situation, made me feel good about myself.

And hence,

The only way we can get our self-respect, self-confidence and self-esteem back is by doing something that gives us a very powerful and positive energy, much much bigger than the negative effects that the incident has caused. It may or may not be related to the incident, but it should benefit a very large population. It could be an inspiration, motivation or an exemplary one.

This book is an endeavour in that direction.

THE TRANSFORMATION

Once we act on the three steps, we will see that the very thought of the act will start bringing positive vibes in us. When we start acting on it, it becomes a commitment, something like our responsibility towards society. The traumatic experience itself turns into a factor of motivation to do it. The inspiration would be so strong that now, we would only concentrate on the task rather than on the experience. We will see that it does not cause much trauma anymore; instead, it brings about a transformation in us. Our body (actions), our mind and our ego will be under our control. The experience, which has been controlling these till now, will no longer be able to control our body, mind, ego and emotions.

This transformation happens because we become the sole controller or manager of our body, mind and ego, and hence, our emotions—the four most important factors that we identify ourselves with—that we get carried away with. We will realise that while we have absolutely no control over outside factors or elements or forces (which includes people, situations and events) that drive us crazy most of the time, what makes us happy and joyous or unhappy and sad is the ability or inability to manipulate these aspects of our life—the body, mind, ego and emotions.

And anything we do for a positive impact on humanity will bring happiness far more satisfying than any other act that one would do to get over such experiences. This truth is very important for all of us to know.

The transformation we would see is that our body heals faster, mind sobers down, ego is subdued and emotions find positive expressions.

STORIES OF PEOPLE WHO HAVE CHOSEN THE THIRD PATH

Many people choose the first path—sulk over the issue, sympathise with themselves, blame something or someone and continue to live their life fighting to put them behind their mind.

Some try to adapt the second path, of revenge, if possible. There is no permanent solution here.

There are people who have knowingly or unknowingly, consciously or unconsciously, chosen the third path and proved that such incidents can actually act as motivation to achieve something big, or something for the betterment of humanity.

Some people who have transformed traumatic incidents in their lives into something bigger are Mahatma Gandhi, Abraham Lincoln, Thomas Elva Edison, Arunima Sinha, Walt Disney, etc. If one types, "People who have fought against odds to success" in the Google search engine, we will find many such achievers.

Everyone might not or need not become famous. But if they can find a way out of such traumatic experiences in their lives, they can find peace, joy and happiness in their life.

Out of the above names, I am tempted to share my views on how two of them used their traumatic experiences to bring out the greatness or uniqueness in them.

Mahatma Gandhi: On the night of June 7, 1893, Mohandas Karamchand Gandhi, a young lawyer then, was thrown off the train's first-class "whites-only" compartment at Pietermaritzburg station in South Africa for refusing to give up his first-class seat. A white man had objected to Gandhi travelling in the first-class coach although he possessed a valid ticket. On subsequent days, he faced more humiliation in his journeys. He even got beaten. A frail thin man that he was, he did not know what to do or how to react. That incident probably must have been the most traumatic experience in his life. Let's see what he did:

1. He let the incident sink in. He accepted it but did not let it demoralise him, nor he did sympathise with himself. He did not let it deter him from trying again.

2. During the same journey, he continued further the next day, again taking a first-class ticket even though he was warned. This time, he was allowed to travel, as his co-passenger did not object.

3. He might have never forgotten this incident. Until then, he wasn't sure what was he doing in South Africa. After the incident, he found a very powerful tool to fight against all discriminations. It was called "Satyagraha." When the whole world was at war, here was a sub-continent with millions of people who stood against a mighty empire with bare hands, blindly following one half-clad frail man on the path of 'Satyagraha.'

Can there be a better example than this to show how a traumatic experience can transform into one that can motivate one for a greater cause?

Arunima Sinha: A national volleyball player from India who was thrown out of a running train in 2011, she had one of her legs amputated lest she die in the hospital itself. She achieved the impossible by climbing the planet's highest peak, barely two years later.

The sequence of events:

On April 12, 2011, Arunima Sinha lost a leg after she was thrown out of a moving train.

On April 12, 2013, Arunima was happy to leave behind the Summit of Island Peak (Height – 6160 metres). She was on her way up to the highest point on the planet.

On May 21, 2013, Arunima Sinha was on top of the world. 8,848 metres above sea level. Mount Everest.

How did she do it?

1. By the time she was taken to the hospital, after a whole night of solitary pain, agony and suffering, she was half-dead. A few days into the hospital stay, she apparently looked at her amputated leg and told her mother, "I want to climb the Mount Everest." **She just accepted the event, not allowing it to make her feel victimised or self-pity.**

2. She turned all her physical, mental, emotional injuries into a challenge that would make her overcome the incident. NOT forgetting it, but by using it as motivation to challenge herself into achieving much beyond her capability at that point in time.

3. Soon, when she was even barely able to walk with an artificial leg, she set about training herself to achieve something seemingly impossible for most people in her place. She, in fact, climbed six of the highest peaks in the six continents by 2014, barely three years after the traumatic experience, and climbed the seventh in 2019.

She is now a social activist and a motivational speaker inspiring people to live powerful lives.

How did I take my third step?

As a normal and common man who suffered a humiliating experience at the hands of a few unknown men who were experts in psyching, tricking and deceiving, I should describe how I decided not to get clawed down by the event.

1. Right from the moment I experienced this, I kept telling myself, "Just accept it as it happened. Don't look for any reason in it. Don't sympathise. Don't feel guilty or ashamed. It happened. It is ok. It has happened." I even kept telling my daughter and her friend to see it that way.

2. Within four days of the incident, I decided to come up with something that would transform this incident into a motivating factor, something more positive and productive—that which would benefit others.

3. I started looking at life more closely. Such experiences happen to most of us.

    a. I started looking at ways to pre-empt them, if at all they were to happen.

    b. Then I tried to see if we could recognise them at least while they were ongoing and if we could pull out before too much damage was done.

    c. And lastly, once they had occurred, what was the best way to live with them for the rest of our lives?

4. And then I wanted to earnestly share this remedy with all in the form of a book. Share how to transform any traumatic experience into one in our favour as a positive experience. This book's intention is just that: **To transform ourselves for more powerful living.**

REITERATION – THIRD STAGE

DEALING WITH THE TRAUMA CAUSED BY THE EXPERIENCE

*We would want to **rewind and erase** some experiences from our memory and life.* But once they have happened, we are left with only three paths to choose from:

First path: Sulk at it and live sulking for the rest of our life, feeling miserable.

Second path: Find someone or something to blame and take revenge, which though gives temporary satisfaction, may not be a lasting solution.

Third path: Transform your life in three steps:

Step 1. Learn to accept it *"as it is."*

Step 2. If possible, try to satisfy the basic instinctive mind by *making good the material or other losses affecting the egocentric identity of the individual.* The very attempt to do so would mitigate the negative effect on the traumatised mind.

Step 3. Tackle the psychological effect by getting *your self-respect, self-confidence and self-esteem back by doing something that gives you very powerful and positive energy that would make the negative effects of the incident look very small.*

EPILOGUE

Our life's journey can be broken down into phases of time frames. The longest journey is from our birth to death. Within that are the smaller journeys of the four stages of growth: childhood, adolescence, adulthood and old age. Each of these stages again has a block of few years to its credit. Each of these blocks of years is made up of days, weeks, months and years. Each day, again, has those seconds, minutes and hours.

When we move from the dimension of time to the dimension of space with respect to our life, we see that every second in time is made up of our actions in space. Actions that are done consciously. These actions or set of actions and their fallout (consequences or fruits) result in experiences. Experiences then divide our life into non-existential past, the existential present and non-existential future. The non-existential past and future 'exist' in our mind while we experience life through our actions in the 'now', that is, in that present moment. Here, the dimension of time (in the mind) and space (through our actions) superimpose each other. The past and future in the mind and the actions, in the present. Both appear real because of the effect they have on each other. And this is life, as we perceive it.

But life is what 'it is.' It is the same for all. The journey makes it unique for each person. How we take it and experience it is based on the impact every moment has on us, which means how it impacts our mind, body and emotions. And ego. Each of us is unique in the way we allow the experiences to impact us. Our identifying ourselves with these three, nay, four aspects of our being, makes up our present, which then lays the foundation for our future. Our past only leaves an impact.

To be more precise:

More often than not, the 'impacts' of our past 'define' our present and lay the 'foundation' for our future. This is how most of us live.

But what is important is that the 'impacts' of the past should be transformed into a 'positive' power in the present, so that the 'foundation' laid now, for the future is 'powerfully positive.'

The End – The start of a new beginning

www.ingramcontent.com/pod-product-compliance
Lightning Source LLC
Chambersburg PA
CBHW031137250726
48655CB00002B/716